Behind the Chutes

Behind the Chutes

ROSAMOND NORBURY

WHITECAP BOOKS *Vancouver / Toronto*

Copyright © 1992 by Rosamond Norbury

Whitecap Books
Vancouver/Toronto

Cover and interior photos by Rosamond Norbury
Edited by Elaine Jones
Cover and interior design by Carolyn Deby
Typography by CompuType, Vancouver, B.C.
Printed and bound in Canada by Friesen Printers, Altona, Manitoba

Canadian Cataloguing in Publication Data

Norbury, Rosamond.
    Behind the chutes
    Includes bibliographical references and index.

    ISBN 1-55110-031-2

    1. Cowboys—Pictorial works. 2. Rodeos—Pictorial works. I. Title.
GV1834.N67 1992   791.8'4'0222   C92-091525-6

For Michael and Mary Norbury,
my mom and dad.

Thank you for never letting me think
I couldn't do it.

Contents

___

Acknowledgments

⸻

For an outsider to gain access to the unique world of rodeo takes special endeavor. For their acceptance and patience with my myriad of questions, Earl Underhill, Sandy and Shawn Chevallier, Jamie Payton, Alison White, and George Tidball are true pals. Of inestimable help with his wit was Brad Goodrich. The late photographer Hank Vogel was an invaluable ally.

By arranging for my first press pass and, five years later, allowing access to her word processor, I'd like to thank Betty Skakum. Of great assistance with words was my equestrian friend, Keltie Kennedy. Helping me along the trail, Dr. Lynne Marie Getz, Christina Beckett, Evelyn Jacobs, Elaine Jones, and the Harts in Ponoka.

To the ineffable Barbara Beeby, a huge thank you for years of friendship, past and future.

*As long as ranching
is a way of life,
rodeo will play a part
in our culture.*

Introduction

Rodeo is living history. Based on a philosophy combining friendship with competition, it embodies the traditions and values of the past. In a world increasingly inundated with a multitude of cheap imitations, the appeal of rodeo is that it is genuine and those who are authentic endure.

Rodeo evolved from the play of the working cowboy. Before the turn of the century, cowboys rode for large cattle outfits, spending months out on the range. To relieve the boredom and monotony of long stretches of time between chores, the cowboys cooked up games to show off the skills they had perfected on the range: cowboying and showing off. Cowboys are known for actions rather than words, so it's tough to get all the facts, but

A lot of guys get started when they borrow something from an uncle or dad, or someone in their family. The next thing you know it's in your blood and you're hooked.

we do know that the first organized rodeo was held in Prescott, Arizona, on July 4, 1888. Admission was charged and prize medals were awarded, a tradition that has evolved to the cowboy's status symbol we know today: the champion's belt buckle.

By the late 1800s William F. Cody saw the entertainment value of bringing the western experience to city dwellers. His Buffalo Bill's Wild West Shows, featuring spectacular live rodeo performances, were largely responsible for creation of the cowboy myth. Urban audiences were given a rendition of the west as seen through the eyes of a showman, a romanticized display of the way the West wanted to be remembered, rather than how it really was. The image of the hard-working, hard-drinking cowboy has also been perpetuated by the press. Quite content to work hard on the range, when the cowboy came to town with his paycheck in hand his natural inclination was to whoop it up and let off a little steam, all observed by people who had never seen him working hard and being responsible. Many cowboys felt they had to live up to their image. Luckily the core of rodeo has remained intact: the working cowboy just doing what he knows best.

The first three decades of this century were hard on rodeo, due to poorly organized events and swindles. Many scenes of violence erupted when cowboys arrived at events promoted by unscrupulous hucksters promising a huge purse, only to find poorly organized affairs with little or no payoffs. It's small wonder that there emerged the image of the fighting cowboy who settled the issues at hand when he arrived from miles of travel to find he'd been fed a pack of lies.

The thirties ushered in a first: cowboys banded together to form an organization. Cowboys are generally loath to join anything, but an association was formed to correct the shortcomings of the crooked and poorly organized promoters. The main grievance was misleading advertising: cowboys often traveled long hard hours to turn up at an event that just didn't pay. These days a cowboy might still not get paid, but that is a result of a bad draw or tough luck rather than cheating promoters. In 1936 the Cowboy Turtles Association was formed to increase prize money and give fair and uniform conditions of competition. There are varying accounts of the name's origin, one being the turtle-necked tops worn to prevent breathing in too much dust. More than likely, though, one of the organizers was quoted as saying, ''We've been slow as turtles doin' something like this.''

In the original cowboy contests, competition was rough. There were no rules to speak of, no eight-second ride; a cowboy rode until he was bucked off or until his horse quit. There was no arena: an open space in town was chosen arbitrarily, with boardwalks and porches forming the confines of the competition area. In some towns competition was outlawed due to excessive damage to the buildings! Women competed along with the men in those early events; until the 1930s they were the stars of the rodeo circuit, as the Cowgirl Hall of Fame in Hereford, Texas, will attest. At the 1929 Pendleton Roundup, Bonnie McCarroll's bronc, Black Cat, fell on her and killed her, and in 1933 Marie ''Ma'' Gibson, a great bronc rider, was killed while performing. These events, along with the small payouts during the Great Depression of the 1930s, led to the decline of women in rodeo.

The Turtles changed their name to the

Rodeo Cowboys Association in 1954, and
finally, in 1975, the organization officially
became the Professional Rodeo Cowboys
Association. As the name indicates, it is
an association of rodeo cowboys that does
not differentiate on the basis of country

or background. It is just as possible for a Canadian or Australian to compete within the organization as an American. As in other professional sports, a cowboy must earn the right to be called a professional by competing in smaller association-sanctioned events and earning points. When earnings total twenty-five hundred dollars on his permit, a cowboy may join the PRCA and compete in larger rodeos. He'll work his way up in the ranks, hoping one day to make it to the National Finals, held in Las Vegas. However, some cowboys are content to continue to compete on the amateur level. Even the most uncoordinated rider, a weekend warrior who racks up years of "fifty-dollar training sessions" without staying on the full eight seconds, can compete. He may be deservedly kidded, but as long as he gives as good as he gets, a rodeo cowboy will never be shut out. This is the wonderful thing about rodeo. Because it is a way of life, cowboys can compete all their lives in the levels of their choice.

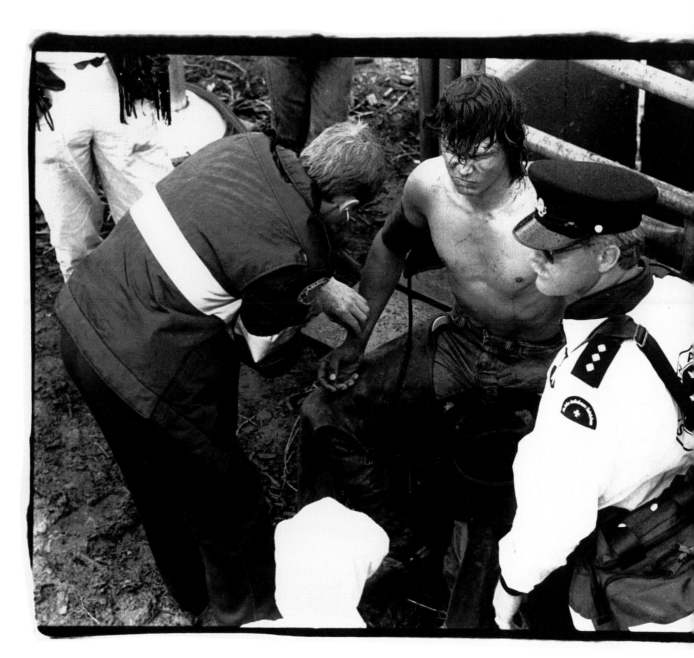

Being a cowboy means having a high pain threshold. This one got bucked off and trampled, so the medical staff is checking him out.

(Opposite) Taking care of family business during the rodeo. Being a cowboy doesn't stop you from being a dad.

A Breed Apart

The word "cowboy" evokes the visual image of a western icon: a high-riding buckaroo with spurs a-jangling, wearing chaps, boots, and a Stetson. But its real meaning is much deeper. It's more the process that goes on inside the package, a state of mind. Cowboy traits include fierce individualism, sheer bull-headedness and a high tolerance for pain. A cowboy believes he can ride any animal he gets up on and catch any calf let out of the chute, that there is no horse or bull that can hurt him or buck him off. The reward is the adrenaline rush rather than the money, fame and adulation, for only a small fraction of cowboys make any real money. Whether it's for the best score, the best seat in the plane or truck, or the date at the Saturday night dance,

A sure sign of spring are cowboys sporting new hats and chaps.

You can tell what event a cowboy specializes in by the shape of his hat. This is a bronc rider: his brim only has a slight curl. Chaps in rodeo are flashier than those on a working ranch, where their use is protection from underbrush and the rain. In rodeo, chaps keep the judge's eyes on your spur action. For this saddle bronc rider they also "keep his swells"—keep him positioned in the saddle.

competition is the very backbone of rodeo and an important part of cowboy life. Yet man against bull or bronc, woman or man and horse against the clock, it's really competition against oneself. Competitors are not in it for the money; it's the steely determination to win that pushes the cowboy on, not the reward at the pay window.

Cowboys can come from just about anywhere: farms, cities, and towns. Their primary source of income is as varied as the individuals involved. A rodeo rider could be a salesman, longshoreman, trucker, schoolteacher, housewife, or rancher. Since the days of Tom Mix and Jim Hart, movie wrangling has been a source of income for many cowboys. It all boils down to the freedom of being your own boss and doing what you love best.

The word "cowboy" is used to refer to both men and women in rodeo. Only women compete in barrel racing, and some women team-rope, chariot-race, and participate in steer undecorating and goat tying. Often heard at the competition are the words of encouragement, "Cowboy up!" It's skill and dexterity in the arena that are the identifying factors, not the gender of the participant.

Rodeo is one of North America's few native sports and it is like no other. There are no managers or holdouts for higher wages: in fact cowboys pay to play. Few sports have athletes lining up for the honor of playing. There is no guaranteed salary, no contract—only the one the cowboy makes with himself. If you count time in the arena, a rodeo rider might physically perform for only forty seconds a year, yet his preparation time is endless. The hours of training and practice, the money put out on entry fees, rental cars, hotel rooms, and on hauling and maintaining the horses becomes a way of life.

Like other members of a professional sport, a cowboy's gear is designed with safety in mind, and he wears the uniform for specific

*A bull rider in old, beat-up boots—
they must be his lucky ones. The
bull's hide can act as a boot jack
and literally pull a boot off, so this
cowboy has his tie-down straps
around his ankles to keep them on.
The rowels are locked so they won't
spin, in order to give a better grip.
Spurs can't hurt a bull, as its hide
is tough, thick and slack.*

reasons. Cowboy boots have evolved through
the years, with the preferred style being round-
toed roper boots. The only place these days
you'll find those pointed toes associated with
the working cowboy are on city streets. In the
event of a wreck, it's best to have the boot slip
off easily, so bull and bronc riders wear a
loose-fitting boot secured around the ankle
with leather thong. Sometimes boots are even
split at the top for faster removal. Heels hold
the foot firmly in the stirrup and the spurs are
more than decoration. For the timed event,
spurs are the cowboy's gas pedal to gun his

horse out of the box, and they are part of the point-gaining process in bull and bronc riding. They must be dull and roweled, and bronc riders' spurs must spin freely. Chaps are a cowboy's identifying logo. They offer a small amount of protection from scrapes and make the ride more attractive from the spectator's viewpoint. With an addition of rosin, they help the saddle bronc rider get a grip on the swells of the saddle. The pearl snaps on a western shirt aren't only for style, but are another safety feature: they are designed to pop open in case a rider gets hung up by his shirt. Bull and bareback riders wear thick leather gloves. Rosin is used to get a better grip as the bareback rider forces his glove into his riggin'. The bull rider also uses the sticky yellow sap on his bull rope to work up a friction in hopes of getting a winning handhold.

The enormous belt buckle, the status symbol of the cowboy, depicts the event in which it was won, the winner's name, and the name and date of the rodeo. A cowboy can amass dozens of buckles over years of performing. But nothing is more sacred to a cowboy than his hat. Each hat is shaped a little differently and each, like the cowboy, has a personality of its own. It offers some protection from the elements, although not from head injuries. (Some claim a cowboy is so hard-headed he doesn't need protection there.) Just about the only time you'll see a cowboy without his hat is during the playing of the national anthems and the reading of the cowboy prayer.

A bareback rider, can of rosin at his side, is working his riggin'. The rosin is sticky and makes it harder for his hand to slip out of the bareback handle during, and sometimes after, the ride. Rosin, a strong arm, and a good sense of balance are the only things that keep him on the bronc's back.

A cowboy's uniform wouldn't be complete without his Wranglers. Tough enough to withstand the spills and scrapes of performing, they are also a cowboy's choice for social occasions such as dances and weddings. The inevitable tin of chewing tobacco is tucked in the rear pocket; husbands and wives can tell their jeans apart by the round mark worn into the fabric.

Being a rodeo cowboy is a strange combination of opposites. Rodeo is the solo sport of absolute individuals, yet cowboys travel with buddies and share with the very people against whom they are competing. Rodeo is friends and family, a sport, a way of life, and a business. To the outsider it's hard to comprehend, but any cowboy can tell you that rodeo gets in your blood, almost like an addiction. It's a craving that can only be satisfied by going on to the next rodeo. No matter how tired and sore he is, how sick and broke, when a cowboy walks into the rodeo grounds anticipating his upcoming event, there is a rush like nothing else under the sun.

It's said if the rodeo doesn't kill you, the commute will.

Preparing for the bull ride, this cowboy wraps the tight-fitting deerskin glove snugly around his hand. The glove acts as a second skin, protecting his hand and keeping it from getting torn up.

(Opposite) Thinking about what's to be done before the saddle bronc ride. Using positive thoughts in getting mentally prepared is an important ingredient of winning.

Ropers start out at an early age; by the time this youngster is ready to compete, his moves will be honed to perfection.

One moment a cowboy

can be cuddling his

daughter and puppy,

the next he's wrangling

rough stock.

(Opposite) So much time is spent on the road that a home-town rodeo is a treat. It's a chance to sleep in your own bed, put buddies up in the spare room and catch up on rodeo videos. These bulldoggers are stopping the action on the VCR to discuss the finer points of steer wrestling and question the judge's call.

A wedding binds the close rodeo ties even tighter.

Cowboys in the wedding party wear their best hats and buckles with new black Wranglers.

Boy steer riders turn up early and watch closely as the older cowboys gear up. Their folks get involved and haul the boys around during the summer months. The boys' role in rodeo is taken seriously: they are the champions of tomorrow.

Nobody can tell more stories than boy steer riders.

Sunday morning the rodeo stands are transformed to an outdoor cowboy church. Christian cowboys can't attend regular church, so the preacher comes to the cowboy. This rancher and guitar picker enjoys rodeo as a fan and uses references to rodeo as illustrations of the gospel for rodeo cowboys and ranchers.

16 Behind the Chutes

Making decisions. Barrel racers pore over the sports news, trying to work out preferred performance days at rodeos they're planning to enter. The phone is close at hand to call the rodeo office. The most organized in the group of traveling buddies is often relied on to plan, call in entries and call back for confirmation.

Cowboy about half an hour before his ride. Shooting the breeze with his buddies, he tries to relax. He wears his glove tucked into his belt until he puts it on just before his event.

Doing a little work outside the rodeo business. In the off-season, this cowboy supports himself by running an excavator.

*Camped out on the couch. On the road a cowboy sleeps
wherever and whenever he can find a spot.*

Roping practice in the home arena. Using a squeaky, clanking replica of a calf, ropers work at a slower speed to analyze the timing and technique needed before turning their attention to the speedier calves.

The beginning of the rodeo performance is one of the few times you'll find a cowboy not wearing his hat. During the grand entry, the flags go by, the national anthem is sung, and the cowboy prayer is recited.

A Breed Apart 21

 Getting warmed up and in the right frame of mind, a bareback rider practices his moves before the event.

(Opposite) Starting out at the rodeo school with an old borrowed suitcase, antique riggin' donated by an uncle, and family spurs. The suitcase will be the first to go, replaced by a softer, all-purpose riggin' bag.

Behind the Chutes

The few organizations in which a cowboy might consider membership are the rodeo associations. These run the gamut from little britches, native, high school, and all-girl rodeos, all the way to prison rodeos. Behind the action in the arena is an administrative core that sees to the smooth and uniform running of the rodeo.

Judges, who have the toughest job, are former rodeo participants and often injured cowboys. They are responsible for judging the performance of both cowboy and stock in rough-stock events on a scale of one to twenty-five for both the cowboy and the animal. A good cowboy on lacklustre stock could receive a lower score than if he had been on impressive stock; however, a true showman can add that extra razzle-dazzle to try for extra points regardless of stock performance. It's up to the luck of the draw when it comes to selection of stock.

That painted-faced man in the arena isn't just any old clown. He's a bullfighter and one of the most important safety features a bull rider has. Whereas rodeo clowns were once over-the-hill cowboys who had seen the bottom of too many whiskey bottles, today they are professional athletes. A bronc will go out of its way to avoid stepping on a thrown cowboy, but bulls are born mad and will make every effort to get at the rider they've thrown from their back. No cowboy takes more chances than a rodeo clown. To protect the cowboy after his ride, he uses only his own body, a fast pair of running shoes and a barrel in which to jump. A good clown can also get the bull to turn in ways that will help a

Paying the entry fees: the worst part of rodeo. Entry fees vary from $25 to $250. A picnic table under a makeshift awning, with rocks to hold down fly-away papers, serves just as important a function as an air-conditioned trailer with a fax machine.

cowboy earn extra points. Entertainers as well, rodeo clowns keep up a running dialogue with the announcer, appear in the audience with a variety of sight gags, and set off impressive pyrotechnic displays in the arena. They alleviate tense moments while medical attention is being given or if bucking stock isn't ready to emerge. In smaller rodeos the bullfighter is sometimes also a participant, so it's not unusual to see a steer wrestler wearing clown makeup waiting on deck for his turn to compete.

Pick-up men are the saviors of the bareback and saddle bronc cowboys. To watch a pick-up man is to see western horsemanship at its finest. They draw alongside the cowboy at the end of his ride to allow him to dismount more easily, remove the bucking strap, rescue a hung-up cowboy, and herd the bronc out of the arena.

The rodeo office is where entry fees are paid and winning checks are handed out. It's probably damp, leaky and full of cobwebs, but it's a place to get news about the performance lineup, find out who's in the lead, and buy dance tickets.

Without the stock contractor, there wouldn't be a rodeo. Theirs is a hard job. They supply stock, making sure it gets to the rodeo on time and is fed and looked after. The contractor and his helpers herd the stock through a complicated series of gates and runways to make sure it ends up in the designated chutes. After the action, the gear is removed and the animals are sorted back to the pens.

The stock contractor is selected for his prime bucking stock. Largely responsible for the smooth running of the rodeo, he makes sure rough stock is in the designated chutes for the start of the rodeo and sees that the timed-event stock is in order according to number down at the other end of the arena. Stock contracting is passed on through generations, with sons and daughters following in parents' footsteps. Contractors are the cowboy's primary source of information on how stock bucks: they know the peculiar characteristics of their stock and willingly share that information. It's good business practice: contractors want a good ride almost as much as the cowboy, as this ensures being hired by the rodeo committee in future rodeos. Stock is specifically bred for bucking characteristics and, like athletes, the horses are recognized at season's end for their talents, with awards such as best bareback or steer-wrestling horse and horse with most heart.

Announcers have a quick wit, smooth voice and encyclopedic rodeo knowledge. They keep the crowd entertained and informed with times, standings, and awards, and they must be able to give the first-time viewer an understandable explanation of the upcoming event while entertaining those attending their hundredth performance. Cowboys are always introduced to the crowd by noting their home town, which remains sacred territory to these modern-day gypsies.

The rodeo office keeps tabs on all financial matters. Making sure all dues are levied and fines paid, overseeing any rule changes and wooing sponsors, office staff are busy throughout the year, although the summer months are particularly hectic. Fines are levied to stock contractors for a variety of infractions, from insufficient stock available to stock not being in the chutes on time. Cowboys can be fined for such behavior as fighting, not wearing appropriate western attire in the arena, or improper handling of stock. When a cowboy phones in his entry, a secretary enters it into a computer. Consideration is given to preferred performance days and traveling buddies, as well as how many rodeos a cowboy will be attending that weekend. The age of computers has facilitated the entry system, but of course this never runs perfectly. There are always the rumblings of dissatisfied cowboys who don't get their choice of days or lineup, but it's more impartial and efficient than the old days when it was done manually.

Rodeo secretaries receive entry money and hand out winning checks. Winnings in each event are determined by the advertised purse, donated by the event's sponsor, plus the total of the entry fees paid in that event. Payoff is dependent on the combination amount of

About an hour before the performance, the stock is drawn. At smaller rodeos the calves and steers are matched up with cowboys by hand; at larger rodeos all stock is drawn in the computer. Cowboys share horses in the timed events, so the judges are figuring out where the splits are: cowboys who ride the same horse don't want to compete back to back.

A lot of time is spent on the telephone. Here at the Calgary Stampede, cowboys are calling in to enter rodeos, find out what stock they've drawn and decide where they're going. Chances are they're calling back to enter rodeos at Cheyenne or Nampa. These are things that have to be done to take care of business.

stock and number of cowboys entered in each event, with prize money going to the top three to five standings in the event. Winning times and scores are taken from all performances of the event over the course of the rodeo.

By doing their particular job, those responsible for running the events often miss the performance. Office staff are busy with details and paperwork. Stock contractors, behind the scenes making sure the stock is loaded right, must rely on cowboys' accounts so they can inform the next rider. Up in the announcer's crow's nest, the timers keep their eyes on the crucial timer's flag, rather than watching the intricacies of the roping or wrestling. Crucial to the rodeo, their love of the sport keeps them there, but they don't get to see the action.

Announcing scores and times, queuing music clips to the action, condensing a lifetime of experiences into a quick quip for the audience, the announcer can make a good rodeo great.

Announcing the rodeo. From his perch in the crow's nest, the announcer must be ready to talk nonstop, keeping a happy-go-lucky attitude that projects a positive feeling and keeps the crowd entertained.

Reading the rodeo news, a saddle bronc rider tries to figure out which rodeo he wants to go to next week and which ones he needs to enter to be in the money. Mandatory reading, it has all the telephone numbers for entries and entry dates, as well as a reference to see how he's placed and how much money he's won. Containing advertisements with photographs of winning rides, tips on sports medicine, and care of animals, sometimes it's the only way to keep informed in the fractured and diverse world of rodeo.

It's balance that

keeps you in the

saddle.

If a horse falls to the ground, the judge will give the cowboy a reride if he didn't disqualify himself before the horse fell. Even after a tumble like this, many take that option.

A saddle bronc rider makes sure his back cinch is right. A friend is holding the buck rein so it doesn't drop down and get tangled up.

*Pick-up men are fearless, fast, and expert horsemen.
They rescue hung-up cowboys and get them to safety,
remove bucking straps, and herd stock from the arena
after the ride, protected only with padded chaps sporting
the sponsor or stock contractor's logo. Pick-up men work
the entire performance; it's exhausting to both horse and
rider and a pick-up man may use as many as four
horses over the course of a performance.*

*With the most injuries of
any event, cowboys joke that
they ride bulls just as an
excuse to meet nurses.*

The bullfighter at work, putting his body and agility on the line against a quicker, stronger, bad-tempered bull. The bullfighter will divert the bull, giving a winded or injured cowboy a chance to run for safety. In protecting the cowboy, this bullfighter is going to take a hooking and probably end up a little sorer than the competitor.

94-657

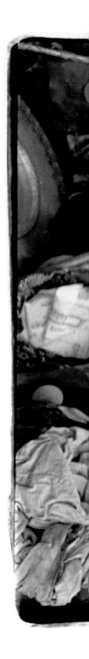

This bullfighter, with lots of hustle and aggression, is trying to turn a bull back. Bullfighters, in addition to protecting the cowboys, compete in an event of their own: spending between forty seconds to a minute in the arena with the bull, they run around the bull, reach out and touch it, and sometimes, for extra points, jump over its back.

He might be wearing makeup, but that's a rough, tough cowboy under the grease paint. A bullfighter prepares his look in his trailer before the performance. In the background are all the sight gags and tricks he'll use to keep the audience amused.

A cowboy flagging rough-stock events. He drops the flag as soon as the front hooves hit the ground, the signal for the timer up in the crow's nest to start the clock. The judges also start their watches when the flag drops and stop timing either when the cowboy gets bucked off or after eight seconds. It's important to get a "clean" flag so there's an accurate time for all cowboys and nobody has to ride for more than their allotted time.

The electric eye: quite possibly the most critical piece of equipment to barrel racers, it is one that causes the most trouble. It seems to take forever to set the timing device, which records the split-second run of the barrel racers, or barrel benders as they're sometimes called.

Some cowboys don't make it to the performance: this is a rodeo-school injury. The student got bucked off and stepped on. His classmates and instructor are trying to take care of him until the medics arrive. It's part of the game, injuries do happen, and this is just one more lesson to be learned at rodeo school.

A little cowboy in training. Mimicking the adults, most of whom carry chewing tobacco, he's playing with a bubble-gum container designed to look like the grownup's tobacco tin.

One way to get involved in rodeo is to compete for the title of rodeo queen. The winner must be able to speak in public and is sometimes called upon to sing the national anthem.

Sharing a joke helps

to relieve the tension

that builds before the

performance.

 Watching the action.

(Opposite) Deep in concentration before his ride, this cowboy is saying a prayer.

Chomping at the Bit

Standing in the rodeo grounds the day before a performance, it is hard to imagine anything could come of this emptiness. The grounds are overgrown with weeds, stock pens empty, chutes and gates closed with last winter's rust. First to arrive on the scene is the stock contractor, hauling those notorious buckers in huge cattle trailers. Steers and calves are leased from local ranchers and arrive the morning of the performance.

Rodeos are generally held over the course of a weekend. Judges, timers, the announcer, secretaries, bullfighters, clowns and crew remain for the duration; competitors drift in and out from rodeos and ranches across the land. Depending on the money up for grabs and the physical logistics of the tour, some have driven all night, while the more fortunate arrive by plane. As the horse trailers pull into the grounds, a feeling of good-natured camaraderie takes over. A cowboy's competitor might just be his babysitter, as everyone lends a hand in keeping an eye on the kids. Contrary to popular conception, not all cowboys drive about in Resistol hats and Tony Lama boots: many arrive in baseball caps and sneakers, but appropriate western attire is required in the arena, so there is a quick change into Wrangler jeans and boots.

The rough stock has already been allocated, so the first order of the day, after the mandatory handshake, is to find out from other cowboys or the stock contractor what to expect: a spinner, a twister, or just an unpredictable bronc or bull. Timed stock is drawn performance day and run down the arena a few times to chart the direction the animals are inclined to take and to let them see where the exit is located. Many hours are spent hanging over the stock pen, sharing points on technique and timing, even knowing that the insight offered might push a share of the purse out of reach.

In the last few hours before performance the arena is busy and noisy with horses being warmed up. Mothers, fathers, uncles often ride with children on the saddle, and the thrill of being in the arena is enough to fuel childhood dreams of future rodeo dramas. Meanwhile, the grounds are readied: the barrier, a marker to give the steer a head start on the cowboy, is set down at the timed-event chutes; the location of the barrels for the barrel race is measured and marked; chute gates are greased; and the arena is harrowed, graded, and watered down if it is too dusty. Most of the visible rocks are removed to make that inevitable fall to the ground just a little safer.

The rodeo office opens a couple of hours before performance. Offices range from air-conditioned buses to temporary tables set up

Modern technology at the rodeo: no more standing in line at the pay phone for call-backs.

46   Behind the Chutes

outside. At the office, entry fees are paid, fines levied and winning checks are cashed; often the winnings are just enough to cover the entry fees.

The use of preventative medicine and the painful reality of riding hurt means a staple of every cowboy's bag are braces and pads and an abundance of surgical tape. Before the performance, cowboys tape hyperextended arms into position; tailbone and knee pads are hidden under jeans, while bruised ribs are left to take another pounding.

During the last fifteen minutes, concentration reaches a peak. Down at the timed-event end there is a calm atmosphere: this competition is one of concentration and precision. Lassos are twirled endlessly and piggin' strings are tied and retied to gain an edge against the clock. Ropers and wrestlers, who share horses in exchange for a percentage of

The maintenance of horses is top priority for winning the timed events. Those who don't bring their own horses to the event use other cowboys' horses for a share of the winnings. This farrier is shoeing his daughter's horse.

Future cowboy watches a saddle bronc rider make sure his stirrups are the right length and feeling comfortable.

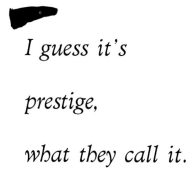

I guess it's

prestige,

what they call it.

the winning purse, do a last-minute check to make sure their hazers and mount horses are arranged. Stock is sorted from holding pens and run through a maze of fences to end up in the chutes. Steers and calves are lined up in order of appearance. The cowboy waiting in the box for his steer to be pointed in the right direction anticipates the perfect combination: horse backed up and ready, steer looking ahead. Foremost on his mind is the unforgiving barrier.

Behind the bucking chutes, cowboys are gearing up: chaps, the cowboy's individual logo, are buckled up, and regulation spurs are strapped on boots. Bareback saddles are whittled to perfection so that the riding glove will fit comfortably in its leather riggin'. Many go through the motions of the upcoming ride, kicking their spurs out, swinging their arm back in a bareback dance all their own. Saddle bronc riders, can of rosin close at hand, are rocking in the saddle, kicking out their boots, going through the riding motion in a saddle on the ground. Bull riders, their riggin' attached to a fence, are rosining their ropes, working up a friction to make the rosin sticky so it will give a better grip. As the cowboys prepare for the final nod to open the bucking chute, loud smacks can be heard, but it's not a fight—just the sound of cowboys slapping themselves to get the adrenaline flowing, to summon the strength for those eight precious seconds in the arena.

For most people, wearing of a brace like this would mean treatment with kid gloves and sympathy; for this rider, it just means he can go on to ride some more broncs.

Ropers are constantly practicing. Everything is fair game: dogs, family, friends, and the old standby—a phony cow's head stuck in a bale of hay.

The secret of success is honing your moves

to perfection.

The rope used to tie the calves is called a piggin' string. It's a six-foot length of quarter-inch rope carried between the cowboy's teeth. Ropers constantly practice tying and retying the string in order to improve their time.

A couple of hours before performance, a rough stock rider arrives at the grounds with the whole family in tow. Carrying his saddle and riggin' bag, he's on his way to the office to pay his entry fees.

Bronc riders, about an hour and a half before the rodeo, take care of business. Making sure nobody has messed with their saddle, getting all rosined up and ready to go, they're discussing the horses they have drawn and which side of the bucking chute they might come out on.

Some of these places,

once a year they're

important and the rest

of the time they're just

wind and air.

While preparation goes on around him, this small cowboy presents a perfect image—from the hat and little roper boots to the pearl snaps on his shirt.

56 Behind the Chutes

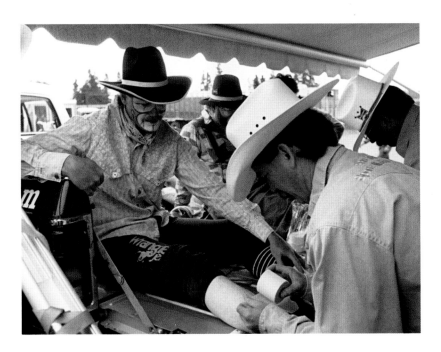

One hour before the rodeo is ready to start, the medical trainers tape the ankles of a bullfighter. He depends a great deal on mobility in the arena and the trainers are practicing preventative medicine, making sure that the stresses and strains aren't going to cause significant injury.

Behind the chutes there's a lot of milling around and activity while waiting for the bulls to be loaded. At right, along the fence, a cowboy is praying, oblivious to the action going on around him.

Start of the grand entry at the Cereal Lions Pro Rodeo. This cowboy, with a fine shiner, is at his second or third rodeo during the fourth of July week (known as Cowboy Christmas because of the abundance of rodeos featured).

A team roper on deck. Team roping is an event that women can enter, and at smaller local rodeos, teams of husbands and wives, sisters, and fathers and daughters compete.

Calf roper, getting ready to ride into the box. In his mouth he carries his piggin' string.

He's preparing himself:

swinging his rope out,

getting loosened up,

thinking about winning.

Arriving at the rodeo grounds, cowboys change from sneakers into boots. The boots will stay on right through to the dance.

Copying his dad's moves, he rocks in the saddle and swings out his arm, imagining the day he'll be old enough to compete.

Chuckwagon racer before the race in Ponoka.

Crash and burn: getting bucked off and hung up. If a cowboy gets bucked over his hand, his body weight forces his hand tighter into the riggin', one of the worst positions to be in. No matter what happens, it'll be painful.

(Opposite) Right before the grand entry, a barrel racer waits with her flag to enter the arena.

The Greatest Show on Earth

The arena is the territory where the cowboy magic is enacted. As the crowd waits with anticipation in the stands and cowboys ready themselves behind the chutes, the rodeo announcer and timers climb into their crow's nest, perched above the bucking chutes. Mounted contestants ride into the arena for the grand entry, each carrying the all-important sponsors' flags and state and provincial flags. As each flag is announced, the rider ''winds a serpentine,'' riding a configuration around the mounted riders until there is a lineup ready for the most solemn moment of the day. Hats are removed, the national anthems are played, and the cowboy's prayer is recited. No matter how many times it's been heard, it can still bring a tear to the eye. As the horses exit the arena, the announcer echos the sentiment on everyone's mind: "Let's rodeo!"

The most common lineup of rodeo events follows a specific order. Bareback riding starts the performance, followed by calf roping, saddle bronc, steer wrestling, team roping, and barrel racing and ending with the grand finale,

Bulls are chosen for their ability to be "rank." A spinning, bucking, hooking, twisting, fighting, kicking bull is marked higher, and the rider is scored on how well he stays in control. Spurring isn't necessary, but will gain more points. Only a strong hand and arm keep the bull rope tight. Balance is most important, as the bull's skin is slippery and it's hard to get a grip with the legs.

bull riding. This order alternates events from one end of the arena to the other, so that as timed events are being run, rough stock is being loaded up at the opposite end of the arena.

There are two major categories of rodeo events: rough stock and timed events. As the name implies, rough stock refers to wild animals: the riding of broncs and bulls. Timed events are competitions where the race is against the clock: calf roping, steer wrestling, team roping, and barrel racing.

There are certain rules that govern rough-stock events. In both saddle and bareback bronc the rider must "mark" his horse, that is, his spurs must be over the break in the horse's neck on the first jump out of the chute. To indicate he is ready for this ride, the cowboy nods for the chute to be opened: any noise would alert the animal, giving it an unfair advantage. In bronc and bull riding, cowboys ride with only one hand and may not touch themselves or their mount during the ride. The cowboy must stay aboard for eight seconds.

Spurs and bucking straps do not inflict pain, but are simply a bother to the animal. It's a popular misconception that the flank strap is cinched around the genital area. Nothing could be farther from the truth. Horses can be mares, geldings or stallions, and the strap, lined with sheepskin and cinched at the flank, is an irritant that encourages the animal to kick higher with its hind hooves. When an animal is hurt it stops dead and certainly will not buck.

The barrier is common to all timed events except barrel racing and is a line marked at the chute opening. The stock must pass the barrier before the cowboy can leave his box

In the team roping, where two contestants work together as they do on a ranch, coordination of the header and heeler is a key element.

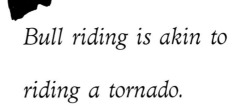

Bull riding is akin to riding a tornado.

The chuckwagon race is a reenactment of camp cooking during roundup. At the sound of the whistle, outriders load poles and a cookstove replica into the chuckwagon. The wagon, pulled by four horses, runs a figure-eight pattern around markers and then races around the track with the outriders pulling behind.

in pursuit. This gives the stock a head start on the cowboy. If the cowboy breaks the barrier, he receives a ten-second penalty.

Bareback bronc was created for the rodeo arena and really bears no relation to ranch work. It tends to be a young man's event and riders are considered to be the temperamental cowboys of rough stock—the mavericks. Some of the wildest action is seen in bareback bronc, which is the most physically demanding of all rodeo events.

Calf roping comes from a long tradition born on ranches. Will Rogers said 75 percent of a roper is his horse, and good roping horses are rented to other cowboys for mount money: a quarter of the winnings. The cowboy backs his horse into the three-sided box next to the narrow chute where the calf is held, then nods to release the animal. The instant the calf passes the barrier line, the cowboy is off in pursuit, throwing his loop to bring down the three hundred pounds of uncooperative, kicking and fighting energy. The clock is stopped when the cowboy throws his hands in the air to signify he has tied the calf.

Saddle bronc is the classic bucking event of rodeo. One of the oldest and most difficult events, it also grew directly from ranch work. It requires that the cowboy supply more equipment than other rough-stock events: an association saddle, a riding glove and a rein. Saddle bronc takes years to learn and the judges look for balance, style, and spurring action.

Steer wrestling is a contest strictly for rodeo, having little ranch application. It matches one man against one seven-hundred-pound steer. The fastest of all events, it can also be the most humiliating if the animal with a rubber neck won't go down, or the cowboy misses the steer altogether and ends up eating dust.

In team roping, the heeler rides out of the box on the right side, the header on the left. The header throws the first loop, catching the steer by the head, and turns it back so the heeler can rope it by the hind legs. A roper's professional life lasts longer than a rider's and many rough-stock cowboys go on to become ropers. Women sometimes participate in this event on the smaller circuits, and team roping becomes a family affair when husbands and wives, fathers and daughters, cousins and in-laws team up.

The only event run regularly in traditional rodeos in which women and girls may enter, barrel racers take a cloverleaf pattern around preset barrels in a race against time.

At the nod of

his head,

the chute opens.

In bareback bronc spurring action, the knees go up and down like piston rods. The ability to use spurs, known as ''good lick,'' demonstrates a cowboy's control over his ride. Whoever spurs highest and hardest will get the best score. Spurring and hand-waving help to maintain balance. The rowels must spin freely, so that they roll over the horse's hide and inflict no damage.

There is a special relationship between barrel racers and their horses; the horse and rider compete and practice as one unit and a barrel racer never lends or shares her horse. In the world of rodeo, barrel racing is a big money winner, owing to the larger number of participants.

Saving the wildest for the last, bull riding is the grand finale of rodeo. It's the most dangerous event and you won't find too many married men competing here! Equipment is simple and cheap: bull rope and bell; glove; fixed, dull, roweled spurs; and lots of rosin. The clangor of the bell on its rope annoys the

This cowboy just got bucked off, and he has either a dislocated shoulder or a problem with his elbow. He's hurting, but he'll be able to "suck it up" and go on to the next ride.

bull, making it buck harder, and the weight of the bell helps drag the rope down when the cowboy releases his grip. It is most dangerous after the ride; a bull will turn on the rider as soon as he's on the ground. This is where the bullfighter plays his crucial role: he's there to distract the bull and protect the cowboy.

Chuckwagon and chariot racing, which are often associated with rodeo, have a circuit all their own. The races are held in the evenings, and there's a festive atmosphere as members of the audience bet among themselves on the outcome of the races, and gear up for the dance.

Not all contestants perform for an audience. If more contestants enter than stock is available the overflow is slotted into "slack," a rodeo performance held late Saturday afternoon or Sunday morning. The ambiance at slack is more relaxed, although the same amount of money is at stake. All those who work the rodeo performance work slack as well, except the entertainment acts. The announcer is present, but since the audience consists largely of rodeo participants, his commentary focuses on in-jokes and inside information.

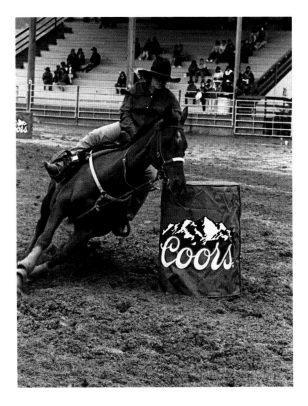

The object in barrel racing is to cut as close as possible to the barrels without knocking them down and run the course in the shortest possible time. The participant brings her own highly trained horse to the event. The racer tries to "get with" her mount, or sit deep in the saddle without moving about, so as not to interfere with the natural running of her horse while it is digging out for the next barrel.

In calf roping, the running horse should be able to "rate cattle," that is, keep the distance between the calf and rider constant, so the cowboy can throw his rope effectively.

Pulled by a team of two horses, three sets of two-wheeled carts race around the track in the chariot race.

Bareback horse throws a cowboy over its head—a quick exit, possibly caused by not using enough rosin.

A complex battle against the clock, thousands of dollars can be won or lost on split-second timing.

In bulldogging, the hazer assists the cowboy in keeping the steer "laned," or running straight and at the perfect distance from the dogger's horse. The bulldogger enters the arena mounted; as his horse catches up with the steer the cowboy scoops his arm under its right horn, allowing it to fit snugly into the crook of his right elbow. He has started to twist before he's entirely free of his horse and as his horse veers off to the left, he rolls out of the saddle, his heels dropping ahead of his body at a forty-five-degree angle to the path of the steer.

The Cowboy Prayer

Heavenly Father, we pause, mindful of the many blessings You have bestowed upon us. We ask that You be with us at this rodeo and we pray that You will guide us in the arena of life. We don't ask for special favors; we don't ask not to draw a chute-fighting horse or never to break a barrier. Nor do we ask for all daylight runs or not to draw a steer that won't lay. Help us, Lord, to live our lives in such a manner that when we make that last inevitable ride to the country up there, where the grass grows lush, green and stirrup-high, and the water runs cool, clear and deep, that You as our last Judge, will tell us that our entry fees are paid. Amen.

A cowboy goes down in the bull-riding event. The bullfighter is doing a good job of distracting the bull from the cowboy, who scrambles away, probably to get on another one tomorrow.

Lift and charge: a saddle bronc rider, showing complete concentration, gets ready to nod his head to open the chute gate.

The saddle bronc wears a standard halter with rope attached, on which the cowboy will mark a handhold by knotting in a piece of mane hair. He holds on with one hand and lifts on the rope to push himself down in the saddle. If the handhold is too short he'll propel himself over the horse's head; too long, and he'll have no lift.

At the start of the wild horse race, competitors wait for the whistle to sound. The chute gates will open, releasing up to eight wild horses into the arena. In this event, cowboys work in teams of three: together they stop their horse, saddle up, and then one team member mounts and rides across the finish line.

The bone-jarring bareback ride can be

compared to riding a jackhammer

with one hand.

The bareback rider must have a powerful grip and a body able to absorb the shock of being whipped back and forth over the horse's back. Sometimes the cowboy's head appears to hit the horse's rump.

In the saddle bronc event,

rhythm is the key to staying on.

In this event, the idea is to get paired up with the meanest animal, one that shows high kicking action, powerful bucking, spinning with changes of direction, and rolling or twisting action.

With his riding face on, a boy steer rider shows his determination. He's not scared but he's a little apprehensive; the older cowboy is there to give him confidence.

The bull wins this round as a cowboy cartwheels in the air before his eight-second ride is over.

 This cowboy just got bucked off, but it's not going to stop him from going to the next rodeo, unless it's really serious. The medics are trying to get him to say his name and the date and make sure he knows where he is.

(Opposite) Electrical therapy and ice help to temporarily relieve the pain after an injury, so this cowboy can go down the road to the next performance.

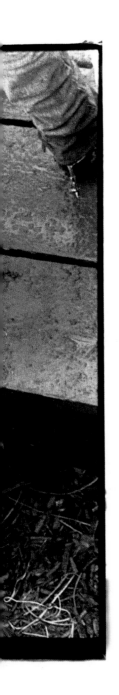

Till the Next Go-Round

The event is complete. All the concentration that's been poured into those few seconds has been transformed to feelings of exhilaration or defeat. Among the cowboys, there is no posturing or strutting, and sometimes it's difficult to determine the leading contestant without knowing the scores.

The psychological tension generated by a cowboy before an event and the rush in the arena mean that adrenaline is still flowing through his system afterwards—and it can be put to use. If his buddy is riding next he'll help with the bucking strap and yell words of encouragement: ''Don't weaken!'' and ''Try, try, try! Go on, try!'' Or there's the beer garden, the site of further ''cowboy contests.'' This is where the bragging, betting, and lying reach a peak.

In some cases, after a cowboy's event is over, he just has enough time to grab his gear and his traveling buddy before moving on to the next rodeo. Many times he'll not see the end of the performance. Yet the event will live on: the stories and reenactment of the competition will fuel many a conversation to come. The retelling of a scene can be strung out far beyond the short duration of the event, with details about the exact turns the bronc took, how the steer was running as it left the chute, what that calf did to escape the expertly thrown rope.

The second most important activity at rodeos, talking to the "buckle bunnies"—rodeo groupies.

Hunger pangs hit once the rush of performance is over. Food at the rodeo grounds is classic Americana: hot dogs, hamburgers, and fries are sold at concession stands organized by the local charity club. Traditional on the rodeo weekend is the pancake breakfast. This is for the audience, but it is also the staple of a cowboy's diet—the cowboy special is two eggs, sausages or bacon, and a stack of pancakes. A cowboy knows that two things can be depended on when he arrives for slack on Sunday morning: there will be a pot of steaming hot coffee with cheap refills, and the pancake breakfast will be served. Eating is generally on the run and a cowboy's stomach must be made of iron, not only to withstand the inevitable tension that accompanies competition, but to be able to digest the fast food and grease that is the road fuel.

The real social center is the area behind the arena, where the horse trailers and campers are parked. There is no organization to the setup—people come and go over the weekend and friends park beside friends. Many gather around the horse trailers to swap information about tack and technique, while racers and ropers make sure their horses are watered and fed. No matter how well or poorly a cowboy does, his horse is always primed and in good condition for the next contest.

If a cowboy's lucky enough to have a hotel room, the television will be tuned to the country music video station. Turns are taken at using the shower and there just may be time for a quick nap after the performance. After a bite to eat at a local steak house, it's on to the Saturday night dance. Dances take place at any location, from the hockey arena to the practice

Killing time, making a little traveling money. You can tell these are rough stock cowboys because they're traveling by car and not hauling horses.

A Texas cowboy rests in his camper after the bulldogging.

barn, where there's dancing on the dirt floor. Cowboys and cowgirls mingle down at one end, still talking about the contest. Single men chase the local girls around. Cowboy lore claims that riding saddle bronc is like dancing with a girl, so the bronc riders are out there moving with the music, getting practice in for the next day's ride.

On Sunday morning the rodeo stands take on a different feeling. The Cowboy Chapter, Fellowship of Christian Athletes, has a strong influence and services are held in the stands, with testimonials from rodeo cowboys. Performers adapt country tunes, using their own lyrics to share their message of faith. Against a backdrop of mounted contestants practicing in the arena, cowboys leaf through the prayer books that are handed out freely at the services.

At the end of the weekend the only sign that the arena once held a swarm of competitors is the trampled grass strewn with discarded surgical tape, coffee cups and tobacco tins.

As the contestants leave, they form mini-convoys. Those traveling in battered trucks drive with confidence, knowing the inevitable breakdown will be fixed by friends who overtake and stop to give roadside assistance and offer spare parts. Some competitors cover more than three rodeos over the course of a weekend. They know when they've reached the halfway point between rodeos as they see friends heading in the opposite direction on the rodeo circuit.

The unquestioning loyalty and bonds between cowboys create a tight-knit but fiercely individualistic family. Loyalty is born out of long trips with traveling buddies. Among these small traveling groups of twos and threes, reserve is broken down over long stretches of monotonous driving and inti-

macies have a chance to develop. As long as
he's whole-hearted, a cowboy will be accept-
ed. After all, if he's not sincere, what is there
to gain from hanging around in the mud, the
blood, and the pain? Rodeo is a test of com-
mitment.

A beer after work.

Life on the road means a lot of quick dining in cafeterias.

Sometimes on a Sunday afternoon, after the last performance of the rodeo, a cowboy must wonder if it's all worth it and think of giving it up. But Monday morning he's back on the phone, putting in entries for the next weekend.

Three generations relax after a day at the rodeo outside Grandma's camper. She can remember driving her son and his buddies in an old station wagon to rodeos in the summer when he was a boy steer rider. Now she's watching him compete in the finals.

After a tough rodeo a cowboy doesn't

need a soft bed in order to fall

asleep.

If there's something to be bet on, a cowboy will bet. These two have had a stack of Coors Light and the match is on for the arm wrestle. One will win, one will lose, but it doesn't matter because they'll buy each other beer later on.

A cowboy is a betting man

always, all times.

Everyone pitches in and helps in times of trouble.

Every rodeo features the Saturday night dance. Generally the participants get together to go over the action of the day, drink, and sometimes even dance.

Everyone has a good time at the dance, even when the facilities are makeshift.

Local dancers kick up their heels.

These cowboys are having a good time at the beer stands—pointing fingers, telling jokes, picking up on women, seeing who can tell the biggest lie.

The pancake breakfast is a staple at every rodeo. The proceeds go to the local charity, with businessmen and celebrities pitching in as cooks. This breakfast is held in the parking lot and entertainment is supplied by the square-dance club.

Rodeo performance

on Sunday is

a staple of

the Christian

cowboy's life.

Cowboying for Christ. The Bible is a strong influence in the rodeo: Genesis 1:28, which calls upon man to have dominion over every living thing that moves on the earth, is at its root.

When the dust has settled it's off to the next ride, to the next town.

If the purse is big enough and the rodeo far enough away, cowboys will pool their earnings and charter a plane. There is just enough space on a small plane to carry essential equipment, with the loser of the coin toss getting the most uncomfortable seat in the tail section.

Rosamond Norbury was born in the foothills of the Himalayas, schooled in Paris, France, and is currently a Vancouver freelance photographer. Her interest in rodeo images has won her much recognition, as her photographs have appeared in many publications including *Westworld*, *Flare*, *Equity*, *Canadian Art*, *Saturday Night*, and *West* magazine. She has been featured on radio and television, and her work has been exhibited in such venues as the Diane Farris Gallery and the Vancouver Art Gallery. *Photo: Jane Weitzel*